W9-AVM-236

SCIENCE
MAGIC
WITH AIR

CHRIS OXLADE

BARRON'S

First edition for the United States, Canada, and the Philippines published 1994 by Barron's Educational Series, Inc.

Design
David West Children's Book Design
Designer
Steve Woosnam-Savage
Editor
Suzanne Melia
Illustrator
Ian Thompson
Model maker
Keith Newell
Photographer
Roger Vlitos

© Aladdin Books Ltd. 1993
Created and designed by
N.W. Books
28 Percy Street
London W1P 9FF

First published in
Great Britain in 1993 by
Franklin Watts Ltd.
96 Leonard Street
London EC2A 4RH

Warning: All activities should be supervised by an adult.

All rights reserved.
No part of this book may be reproduced in any form by photostat, microfilm, xerography, or any other means, or incorporated into any information retrieval system, electronic or mechanical, without the written permission of the copyright owner.

All inquiries should be addressed to:
Barron's Educational Series, Inc.
250 Wireless Boulevard
Hauppauge, NY 11788

International Standard Book No.
0-8120-6444-5 (hardcover)
0-8120-1983-0 (paperback)

Library of Congress Catalog
Card No. 94-5547

Library of Congress Cataloging-in-Publication Data

Oxlade, Chris.
Science magic with air / Chris Oxlade. — 1st ed. for the U.S., Canada, and the Philippines.
p. cm. — (Science magic)
Includes index.
ISBN 0-8120-6444-5. — ISBN 0-8120-1983-0 (pbk.).
1. Conjuring—Juvenile literature.
2. Air—Juvenile literature.
[1. Magic tricks. 2. Air.
3. Scientific recreations.] I. Title.
II. Series.
GV 1548.095 1994   94-5547
793.8—dc20   CIP
                                  AC

Printed in Belgium
4567 4208 987654321

CONTENTS

J793.8 0982 C.1

BE AN EXPERT MAGICIAN	6
SELF-INFLATING BALLOON	8
JUMPING COIN	10
AMAZING HOVERCRAFT	12
ROLLING BALL	14
MAGIC HELICOPTER	16
SINKING SQUID	18
HOVERING BALL	20
NONBURSTING BALLOON	22
RISING TIDE	24
ASTONISHING EGG	26
HINTS AND TIPS	28
GLOSSARY	30
INDEX	30

AIR MAGIC!

Because air is invisible, you may forget that it is all around us all of the time. But there's magic in the air, and each trick reveals another of its amazing qualities. Air is made up of many gases that are essential to life on Earth. It can be squeezed into very small spaces, and it will expand when heated. Air can move around, and even has the power to support other objects. It is a magnificent, show-stopping magic prop.

BE AN EXPERT MAGICIAN

PREPARING YOUR ROUTINE

There is much more to being a magician than just doing tricks. It is important that you and your assistant practice your whole routine lots of times, so that your performance goes smoothly when you do it for an audience. You will be a more entertaining magician if you do.

PROPS

Props are all the bits and pieces of equipment that a magician uses during an act, including his or her clothes as well as the things needed for the tricks themselves. It's a good idea to make a magician's trunk from a large box to keep all your props in. During your routine, you can dip into the trunk, pulling out all sorts of equipment and crazy objects (see Misdirection). You could tell jokes about these objects.

PROPS LIST

Magic wand ★ Top hat ★ Vest
Aluminium foil ★ Balloons
Bendable drinking straw
Cellophane tape ★ Colored
cardboard ★ Colored paper ★ Eggs
Egg carton ★ Glass jars, large and small
Glue ★ Large cardboard box ★ Large, flat
glass container ★ Large needle ★ Marble
Modeling clay ★ Paints, some oil based ★ Paper clip
Party candle ★ Pencil ★ Ping-Pong ball ★ Pins
Pitcher ★ Plastic lid ★ Plastic soda bottles, one with
cap ★ Plastic tubing ★ Polystyrene ★ Rubber bands
Scissors ★ Sheet of plastic ★ Silk handkerchief
Small coins ★ Small dish ★ Sticky putty ★ String
Undersea scene ★ Vacuum cleaner ★ Water

WHICH TRICKS?

Work out which tricks you want to include in your routine. Put in some long tricks and some short tricks to keep your audience interested. If you can, include a trick that you can keep going back to during the routine. Magicians call this a "running gag."

MAGICIAN'S PATTER

Patter is what you say during your routine. Good patter makes a routine much more interesting and allows it to run more smoothly. It is a good way to entertain your audience during the

slower parts of your routine. Try to make up a story for each trick. Remember to introduce yourself and your assistant at the start and to thank the audience at the end. Practice your patter when you practice your tricks.

MISDIRECTION

Misdirection is an important part of a magician's routine. By waving a colorful scarf in the air or telling a joke, you can distract the audience's attention from something you'd rather they didn't see!

KEEP IT SECRET

The best magicians never give away their secrets. If anyone asks how your tricks work, just reply, "By magic!" Then you can impress people with your tricks again and again.

INTRODUCING MAGIC MANDY
AND THE
SELF-INFLATING BALLOON
The balloon inflates by itself as Magic Mandy has a fit of sneezing!

WHAT YOU NEED
Scissors ★ Plastic tubing Balloons ★ Rubber bands ★ Silk handkerchief

Reach beneath your magic table and pretend to take hold of a balloon. As you do, secretly pull the balloon from one sleeve and the tube from the other. Hide the tube by picking up the handkerchief. Now pretend to sneeze into the handkerchief (but secretly blow strongly into the tube). With a real blast of air, the balloon will inflate!

THE SCIENCE
BEHIND THE TRICK

When you blow out, the air is squeezed inside your lungs. This increases the pressure of the air, making it higher than the pressure inside the balloon. Air always moves from an area of high pressure to an area of low pressure, so it rushes along the tube to the balloon. A balloon is difficult to inflate because you have to stretch the rubber by using the air pressure in your lungs.

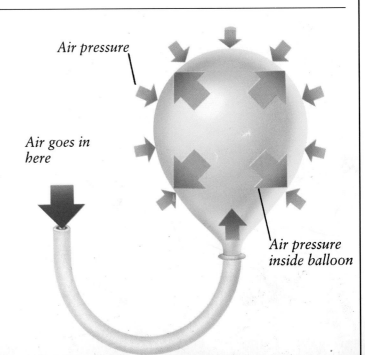

Air pressure

Air goes in here

Air pressure inside balloon

1 Cut a piece of plastic tubing long enough to go up one sleeve, around your back, and down the other sleeve.

2 Stretch the neck of a balloon over one end of the tube. If it's loose, wind a rubber band tightly around it. Feed the tube along your sleeves.

3 Put rubber bands around your wrists (not too tightly) to hold the tube in place.

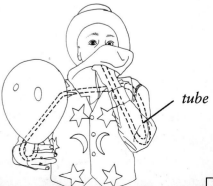

tube

9

INTRODUCING MAGIC MALCOLM
AND THE
JUMPING COIN

Magic Malcolm makes the coin jump in an amazing feat of mind over matter.

Let your audience inspect the coin and the bottle to prove that there is nothing "tricky" about them. Put the coin over the top of the bottle (remember to wet it secretly first). Now put your hands gently on either side of the bottle, and the coin will begin to jump!

WHAT YOU NEED
Large plastic soda bottle Oil-based paint ★ Small coin ★ Small dish of water

THE SCIENCE
BEHIND THE TRICK

Your hands are warmer than the bottle and the air inside it. Heat always flows from a warmer place to a cooler place. When you put your hands on the sides of the bottle, heat flows from your hands into the bottle and warms the air. When air gets hotter, its tiny particles (molecules), move around faster as it expands. The water seals the area around the coin to stop air from leaking out. The expanding warm air breaks the seal, and the coin flips up to let some air escape. Then the coin falls back down until the air expands again.

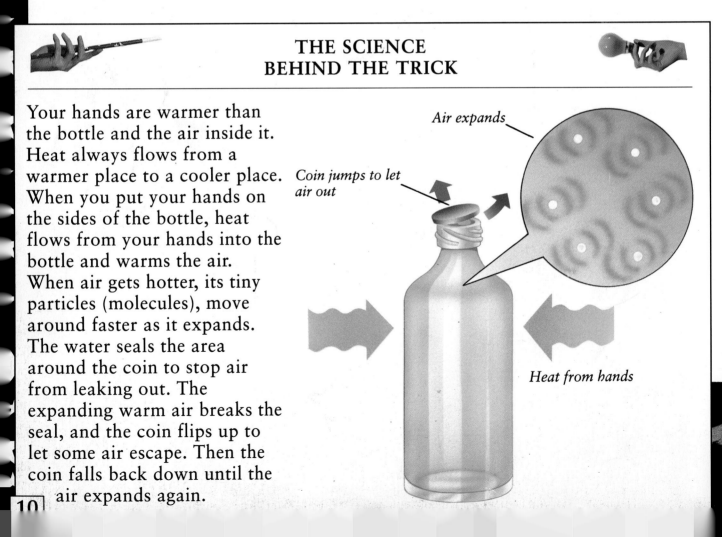

Air expands

Coin jumps to let air out

Heat from hands

Paint the bottle with the oil-based paint. Find a coin that just covers the top of the bottle. Keep the small dish of water hidden away, and dip the coin in it just before you perform the trick.

INTRODUCING MAGIC MARCIA
AND THE
AMAZING HOVERCRAFT

Only Magic Marcia has the power to make this strange craft float along.

Put the hovercraft in the center of your table. Invite members of your audience to come forward and try to move the craft by blowing. It will refuse to move. Ask your volunteers to stand back. Now blow sharply into the hole at the top of the hovercraft, without touching it, and it will glide smoothly across the table!

WHAT YOU NEED
Plastic bottle ★ Colored cardboard ★ Colored paper ★ Sticky putty

THE SCIENCE
BEHIND THE TRICK

It's difficult to blow the hovercraft along because of friction between its "skirt" and the table. When you blow into the hole at the top, air gets squeezed inside. This makes a "cushion" of air underneath which lifts the hovercraft off the table so that it can float along.

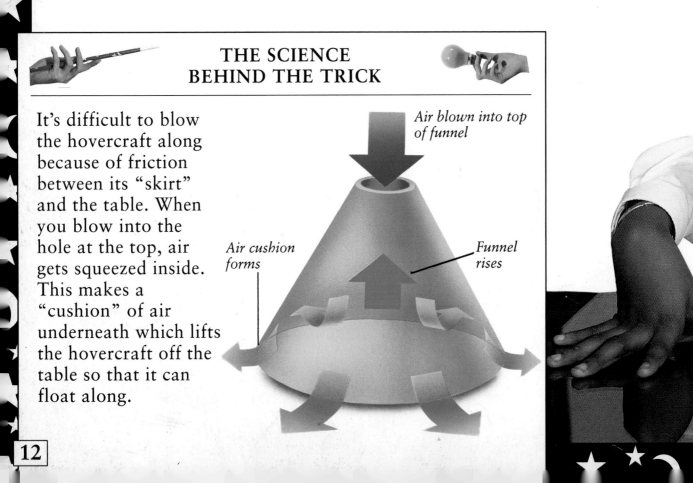

Air blown into top of funnel

Air cushion forms

Funnel rises

1 Cut 2 in. (5–6 cm) off the top of the plastic bottle to make a funnel.

2 Make a "skirt" to fit over the funnel. Cut a semicircle of cardboard and decorate it as shown. The skirt must fit exactly with the bottom edge.

3 Fold the skirt around the top of the bottle, and glue it into place.

4 If the hovercraft moves too easily, add some sticky putty underneath.

WHAT YOU NEED
Spray can lid ★ Scissors
Balloons ★ Cellophane
tape ★ Large glass jar
Colored paper or paints
Marble

INTRODUCING MAGIC MALCOLM
AND THE
ROLLING BALL

Magic Malcolm's wand focuses the mind power of the audience to make the mysterious ball roll.

Rest your hand on top of the glass jar and point your wand at the marble. Tell the audience that they can move the ball just by mind power. Ask them to look at the ball and concentrate hard. Secretly press the balloon on the glass jar and they will think they are moving the ball!

THE SCIENCE
BEHIND THE TRICK

Air is trapped inside both the containers. When you press on the balloon, the air inside the large container gets squeezed. Its pressure goes up. Now the pressure outside the small container is greater than inside. The air outside pushes in the balloon on the small container, and the marble rolls toward the center.

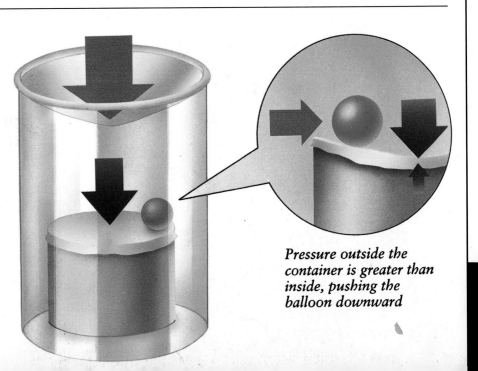

Pressure outside the container is greater than inside, pushing the balloon downward

1 Find a plastic lid about 1½ in. (4 cm) across. Make sure that there are no holes in it because it needs to be airtight.

2 Cut the neck off a balloon. Stretch it over the lid so that it's tight, like a drum. Use the tape to make an airtight seal around the edges and to keep the balloon in place.

3 Now find a large, strong glass jar (e.g. a coffee or pickle jar). Make sure that it's big enough to hold the lid.

4 Decorate the lid, and put it in the glass jar with the marble on top. Seal the glass container by stretching another balloon over the top. This is the part that you will press.

WHAT YOU NEED
Cardboard ★ *Scissors*
Cellophane tape
Needle ★ *Aluminium foil*
Jar of warm water

INTRODUCING MAGIC MIKE
AND THE
MAGIC HELICOPTER

No motor? That's no problem for Magic Mike as he makes the helicopter work by magic.

Place the helicopter on the cylinder without the jar inside, and put the rotor on. The rotor will stay still. Now move the helicopter to the other cylinder and wave your wand. This time the rotor will turn — and keep turning! Make this the first trick in your routine and the rotor will still be turning at the end.

THE SCIENCE
BEHIND THE TRICK

The water in the jar gives off heat, which warms the air around it. The tiny particles in the air (called molecules) move faster, making the air expand and become less dense. The warm, light air floats upwards in the cool, heavier air around it, just as light things float in water. The stream of warm air flows out of the cylinder, making a light wind that moves the rotor. The rotor keeps going until all the heat in the water is used up and the air around it stops being warmed.

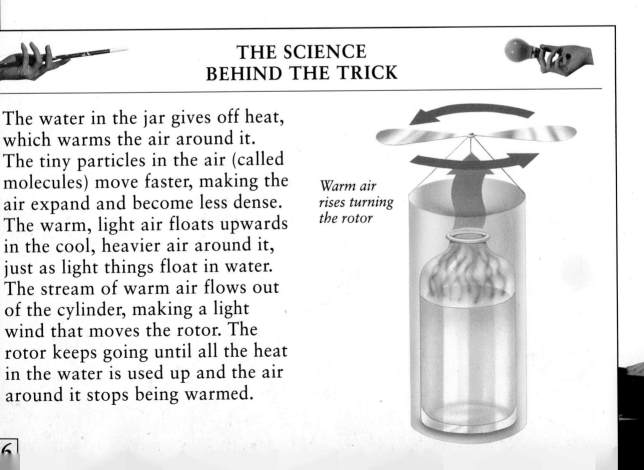

Warm air rises turning the rotor

1 Draw a helicopter shape onto the cardboard and cut it out. Tape a large needle to the back with the point at the top.

2 Cut a rotor shape out of the aluminium foil. Shape it so that it balances on the needle. From the cardboard make two cylinders each about 12 in. (30 cm) high and big enough to hold a jar of warm water.

3 Just before starting your routine, put the jar of warm water into one of the cylinders.

INTRODUCING MAGIC MARCIA
AND THE
SINKING SQUID

Going up! Going down! The little squid rises and sinks at Magic Marcia's command.

This trick gives you a good opportunity for some funny patter. Perhaps you could start with "This squid has baffled the world's greatest scientists. . . ." Squeeze the bottle to make the squid sink, and let go again to make it float!

WHAT YOU NEED
Scissors ★ Plastic Bendable straws Sticky putty ★ Paper clips ★ Glue ★ Under-sea scene ★ Plastic soda bottle ★ Water

THE SCIENCE BEHIND THE TRICK

When you squeeze the bottle, you are trying to squeeze the water and air inside. Water cannot be compressed, but air can. When the air inside the model is compressed, more water can enter, making the squid heavier, so that it sinks.

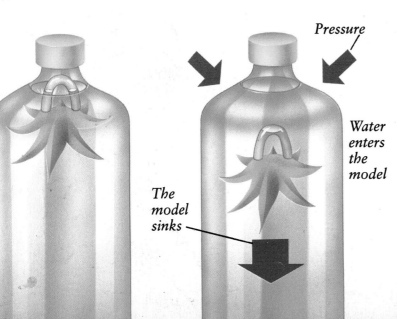

Pressure

Water enters the model

The model sinks

1 First, make the squid model. Cut tentacles from the plastic. Cut the ends from the straw, and bend it in the middle. Join the straw, plastic, and sticky putty with the paper clips as shown.

2 Glue the undersea scene on the bottle. Test the squid in water to see that it just floats. Add or remove sticky putty until it does. Fill the bottle with water, put in the squid, and put on the cap.

INTRODUCING MAGIC MARCIA
— AND THE —
HOVERING BALL

The ball seems to be attached to Magic Marcia's wand by an invisible force!

Hold the ball above the center of the box while your assistant secretly pushes the vacuum hose into the hole. Now make the ball move by saying "left" or "right." Your assistant listens and moves the hose accordingly so that it looks as though the ball is under your control. At the end of the trick, your assistant pulls the hose away very quickly and you show the empty box.

WHAT YOU NEED
Large cardboard box
Colored paper ★ *Scissors*
Quiet vacuum cleaner
(that can blow as well as
suck) ★ *Ping-Pong ball*

THE SCIENCE BEHIND THE TRICK

The stream of air pushes the ball into the air. The air flows all around the ball as it hovers. If the ball moves sideways, more air flows around one side than the other. This creates a pull on the ball, and it returns to the center of the stream. It works like an aircraft wing. It even works when the stream of air is at an angle.

Air stream

Ball moves from side to side but remains in the center

1 Decorate the large cardboard box. Cut a slot in the bottom large enough for the vacuum hose to fit through.

2 Turn the vacuum on to blow. Before your routine, hide the vacuum and your assistant under your magic table. Be sure your assistant is facing the audience.

Ball

Box

Vacuum cleaner

23

WHAT YOU NEED
Balloons ★ String
Cellophane tape
Scissors ★ Pin

INTRODUCING MAGIC MARK
AND THE
NONBURSTING BALLOON

Magic Mark astounds the audience with a trick that doesn't go off with a bang!

Pick up one of your prepared balloons and show it to the audience. The cellophane tape will be almost impossible to see. Now push a pin into the balloon through the tape. Your audience will probably flinch because they think the balloon is going to burst! Take out the pin, and quickly insert it in another spot to burst the balloon and destroy the evidence.

THE SCIENCE
BEHIND THE TRICK

When a balloon is blown up, the rubber is stretched. Inside the balloon, the air is compressed. When you stick in a pin, you start a tear in the rubber. Faster than the eye can see, the tear spreads and all the air rushes out, making a bang. In this trick the tape stops the tear from spreading.

Tear spreads

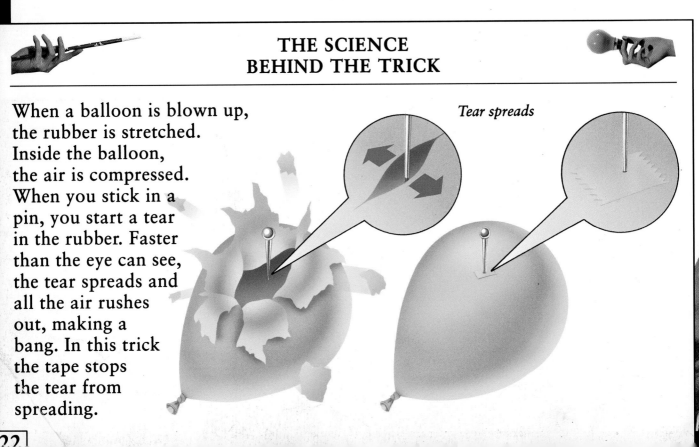

This trick is quick and easy to prepare for. It's best to prepare two or three special balloons just in case something goes wrong! Blow up each balloon and tie the neck. Cut a piece of tape about 1 in. (2 cm) long, and stick it near the top of the balloon. Smooth it down carefully so that it's difficult to see.

INTRODUCING MAGIC MANDY
AND THE
RISING TIDE

Even the ebb and flow of the tide is under Magic Mandy's spell!

WHAT YOU NEED
Large flat glass container
Small coins ★ Glass jar
Pitcher of water
Scissors ★ Polystyrene
Glue ★ Party candles

Slowly pour the water into the large container. Float the boat above the coins, and light the candle. Announce that you will make the tide rise under the boat. Place the glass jar over the boat so that it rests on the coins. The water will begin to rise!

THE SCIENCE BEHIND THE TRICK

When something burns, it uses up oxygen in the air. In fact, without oxygen, things cannot burn at all. When you put the jar over the boat, the oxygen inside is gradually used up and the candle goes out. The air pressure on the water in the large container pushes water up into the jar so that the boat rises.

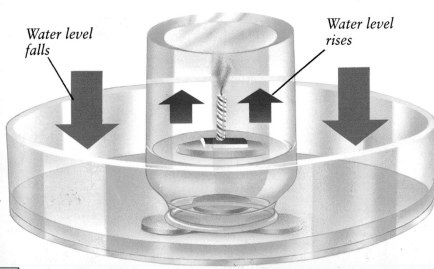

Water level falls

Water level rises

1 The large glass container shown here is ideal. If you don't have a glass container, you can use a shallow tray or a large plate.

2 Put three small coins in the middle of the container, and space them out so that they will support the glass jar when it is turned upside down. Pour some water into a pitcher.

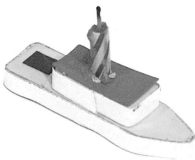

3 Cut out two pieces of polystyrene, as shown, and glue them together to make a boat. Attach the small candle to the top.

INTRODUCING MAGIC MALCOLM
AND THE
ASTONISHING EGG

And finally. . . Magic Malcolm has his audience diving for cover with another egg-citing trick!

This trick gives you a good opportunity for some funny patter. Perhaps you could start with "These are the rare and valuable eggs of an extinct bird. . . ." Open the egg box, take out an egg, and throw it hard at the ceiling. Your audience will think they are about to be covered with egg, but a parachute will float down instead.

WHAT YOU NEED
Pin ★ Eggs ★ Four pieces of string ★ Silk handkerchief Modeling clay ★ Egg carton ★ Colored paper or paints

THE SCIENCE BEHIND THE TRICK

When an object falls through the air, the air tries to slow it down. This is called drag or air resistance. When your parachute begins to fall, the drag on the object is much less than on the handkerchief. The object falls faster, pulling the parachute open. When the parachute is open, its drag is much greater so it slows down and floats to the ground.

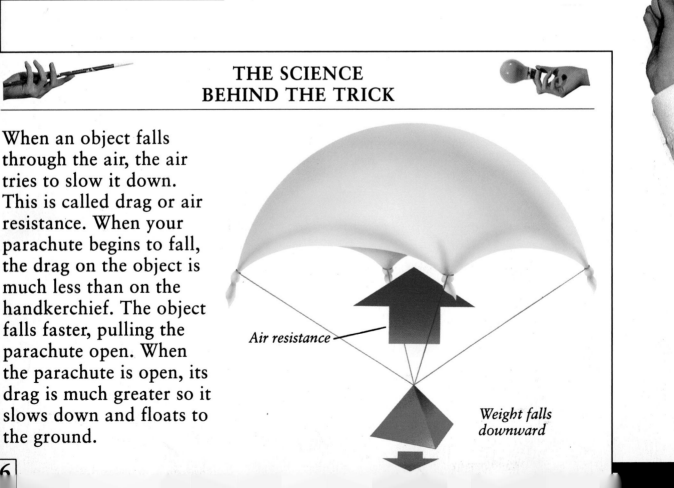

Air resistance

Weight falls downward

2 To make a parachute, tie a piece of string to each corner of the handkerchief. Wrap a piece of modeling clay around the strings.

1 Using the pin, carefully make a small hole in the end of an egg. Gradually make the hole big enough to wash out the white and yoke. Prepare several eggs the same way.

3 Carefully push the parachute into one of the eggs. Be careful not to tangle the strings. Decorate the egg carton to keep your eggs in.

HINTS AND TIPS

Here are some hints and tips for making your props. Good props will make your act look more professional, so spend time making and decorating your props, and look after them carefully. As well as the special props you need for each trick, try to make some general props such as a vest and a magic wand.

Decorate your props with magic shapes cut from colored paper. Paint bottles and tubes with oil-based paint.

You will need cellophane tape and glue to make props. Double-sided tape may also be useful. You can use sticky putty or special plastic sealant to make waterproof joints.

Try cutting magic shapes out of cardboard and using the holes to make stencils.

Your act will look more professional if you make a stage setting. This is easy if you have a backdrop to hang behind the stage. A large piece of black cloth is most effective. Use silver paint to create stars and moons. Also decorate pieces of cloth to throw over your table. The overall effect will be dramatic, creating an atmosphere of mystery and magic.

Make your own magician's clothes. Try to find an old hat and vest to decorate. If you can find some silvery material, cut out stars and moons and sew them on. An alternative is to use sequins or anything else that is shiny and dramatic so you look professional.

Table

Backdrop

Cloth

Assistant's table

Make a magician's table by draping a cloth over an ordinary table. You can put the props out of sight underneath.

GLOSSARY

AIR PRESSURE The force exerted on the surface of objects because of the squeezing or pressing of air.

AIR RESISTANCE The drag or resistance that air exerts on falling objects. The larger the surface area of an object, the greater the air resistance.

BURNING The consumption of oxygen in the air to release heat energy from certain materials.

COMPRESSION The squeezing together of particles as a substance moves into a smaller space. As air is compressed, it exerts a higher pressure on the surrounding container.

FRICTION A force that exists between two objects in contact and resists relative motion between them. Air can sometimes act as a lubricant, reducing the friction between two surfaces.

MOLECULES The smallest naturally occurring particles of a substance.

OXYGEN A gas without taste, color, or smell that forms a part of air. It is essential to life on Earth.

INDEX

air cushion, 12
air pressure, 8, 14, 18, 24
air resistance, 26
airstream, 20
airtight, 15
Amazing Hovercraft, 12–13
Astonishing Egg, 26–27

backdrop, 29
balloon, 8, 9, 14, 15
boat, 24–25
burning, 24

candle, 24–25
cellophane tape, 22, 23, 28
coin, 10, 11
cylinder, 16, 17

double-sided tape, 28
drag, 26

egg, 26–27
expanding, 10

floating, 26
friction, 12
funnel, 12, 13

heat, 10, 16
high pressure, 8
hints and tips, 28–29
hose, 20
Hovering Ball, 20–21

invisible force, 20

Jumping Coin, 10–11

low pressure, 8

Magic Helicopter, 14–15
magician's clothes, 29
magician's patter, 7
magician's table, 29
misdirection, 6, 7
molecules, 10, 16

Nonbursting Balloon, 22–23

oil-based paint, 11
oxygen, 24

parachute, 26
patter, 7, 18, 26
plastic bottle, 10, 11, 12, 13

plastic sealant, 28
props, 6, 28, 29
props list, 6

Rising Tide, 24–25
Rolling Ball, 14–15
rotor, 16, 17
routines, practicing, 6
rubber bands, 9
"running gag," 7, 18

secrets, keeping, 7
Self-inflating Balloon, 8–9
sequins, 29
Sinking Squid, 18–19
stage set, 29
squeezing, 12, 14, 18

tear in rubber, 22
tricks, choosing, 7

vacuum cleaner, 20, 21

wand, 14
wind, 16

CHICAGO HEIGHTS PUBLIC LIBRARY